You're Officially A Grown-Up

The Graduate's Guide to Freedom, Responsibility, Happiness, *and Personal Hygiene*

Judith Viorst

Illustrations by Robin Preiss Glasser

Simon & Schuster

SIMON & SCHUSTER
Rockefeller Center
1230 Avenue of the Americas
New York, NY 10020

Manufactured in the United States of America

1 3 5 7 9 10 8 6 4 2

Library of Congress Cataloging-in-Publication Data
Viorst, Judith.
You're officially a grown-up : the graduate's guide to freedom,
responsibility, happiness, and personal hygiene / Judith Viorst ;
illustrated by Robin Preiss Glasser.
p.   cm.
1. High school graduates—Poetry. 2. College graduates—Poetry.
3. Young adults—Poetry. 4. Adulthood—Poetry. I. Title.
PS3572. I6Y6   1999
811'.54—dc21   98-31535
                                      CIP
ISBN 0-684-85342-6

For Marla Rigel, Marya Gwadz, and Jeannette Luoh
—J.V.

For my sister Jacqueline, with love
—R.P.G.

YOU'RE OFFICIALLY A GROWN-UP

You're going.

You're leaving.

You're out on your own.

If your buttons fall off
And you must have them sewn,

You must sew them yourself.

You're officially a grown-up.

You'll balance your checkbook,
Remember to vote.
You will write your Aunt Frances
A prompt thank-you note,

And take out the garbage
And sweep up inside—

Or not. From now on
It is you who'll decide
What you will and won't do.
You're officially a grown-up,

Which means you can sleep
On the same grubby sheet
From September to June,
Eat whatever you eat

Without someone saying,
"You call that a meal?"
(Or, if you don't eat,
Asking, "How do you feel?"

As if you are catching
Some fatal disease).
You can do as you please.
You're officially a grown-up.

You can do as you please, but please keep in mind
That if you don't water your daisies you'll find

That you're likely to wind up with a lot of dead flowers.

You can do as you please, but please be aware
That people who don't change their underwear

May be lonelier people than those who take regular showers.

You can stay up all night.
You can snooze the whole day

As long as you've figured out
How you will pay
For the stuff that you need.

You're officially a grown-up.

You can hang by your toe
Off a ninety-foot drop,
Because nobody's standing there
Hollering, "Stop!"

And you needn't show up,
And you needn't call in,
Because nobody's wondering
Where you have been.

(Don't they *care* where you've been?)
You're officially a grown-up,

Which means you should have
All the answers. (You won't.)
And always know what
You are doing. (You don't.)

And never behave like
A wimp or an ass.
(You will, but the shame
Does eventually pass.)
Are you worried? Confused?
You're officially a grown-up.

And you're going.
You're leaving . . .

Or maybe you'll stay
One more week, one more month,
Or perhaps till next May.
What's the rush? Just because
You're officially a grown-up?

Yes, what is the rush?
You've got room, you've got board,
And no charge for the phone,
And the keys to the Ford,

A deck you can tan on,
A big-screen TV,
And that soft teddy bear
You have owned since age three.
(But you aren't age three.
You're officially a grown-up),

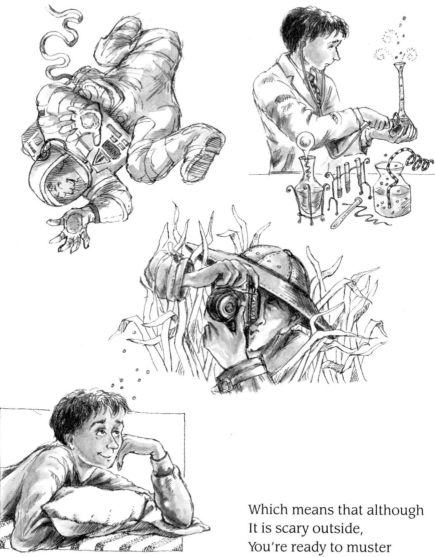

Which means that although
It is scary outside,
You're ready to muster
Your courage and pride,
To hold up your head,
Boldly stick out your chin,

And—fall flat on your face
And come up with a grin,
Determined and dauntless
(And shaky, you say?
You'll move on, anyway).
You're officially a grown-up.

And no matter how shrewdly your plans are made,
It sometimes will rain on your parade,
And you'll have to slog through the rain,
Though you hadn't planned to.

And adorable creature though you may be,
You won't be everyone's cup of tea,
For not everyone you meet is going to
Love you,
Or like you,
Or want to understand you.

Still, you're going.
You're leaving.

You're ready to take
On your future.
This could be a major mistake.
So you'll make a mistake.
You're officially a grown-up.

You'll try on this hat.
And you'll try on that role.

And you'll learn what you can
And can never control.

You'll bail yourself out
If you get in a jam.

You'll, when asked who's in charge
Of your life, say, "I am."
And you are. Yes, you are.
You're officially a grown-up,

Which means you can still
Call for help when you're stuck.

You can count on good friends.
You can hope for good luck.

And you might cross your fingers.
You might say a prayer.

But it's you—mostly you—
Who will get yourself where
You'll, sooner or later, decide
That you're trying to get.

Will you get there? You bet!
You're officially a grown-up.

Judith Viorst is the author of eight collections of poems, six books of prose, and twelve children's books, including the classic *Alexander and the Terrible, Horrible, No Good, Very Bad Day.* She lives in Washington, D.C., with her husband, Milton, a political writer. They have three sons—Anthony, Nicholas, and Alexander.

Robin Preiss Glasser has illustrated a string of long-titled children's books, including *Alexander, Who's Not (Do You Hear Me? I Mean It!) Going to Move,* by Judith Viorst, and *You Can't Take a Balloon into the Metropolitan Museum.* A professional ballet dancer for twelve years, she is the mother of Sasha and Benjamin. She lives in Newport Beach, California.